THE COOK'S COLLECTION

CAKES
&
COOKIES

Author: Annette Wolter
Photography: Odette Teubner and Susi and Pete Eising
Translated by UPS Translations, London
Edited by Josephine Bacon

CLB 4152
This edition published in 1995 by Grange Books
an imprint of Grange Books PLC, The Grange, Grange Yard, London SE1 3AG
This material published originally under the series title "Kochen Wie Noch Nie"
by Gräfe und Unzer Verlag GmbH, München
© 1995 Gräfe und Unzer Verlag GmbH, München
English translation copyright: © 1995 by CLB Publishing, Godalming, Surrey
Typeset by Image Setting, Brighton, E. Sussex
Printed and bound in Singapore
All rights reserved
ISBN 1-85627-785-2

THE COOK'S COLLECTION

❋

CAKES
&
COOKIES

Annette Wolter

Grange
BOOKS

Introduction

Home-baked cakes and biscuits are marvellous! A freshly baked cake is always an indication of goodwill, of wanting to share, and of wanting to be sociable. The same goes for luscious, freshly baked, crumbly biscuits. Both cakes and biscuits taste so much more wholesome without all those additives, preservatives and artificial colourants found in commercially made foods.

Whether you are looking for a special party cake as the centrepiece for a buffet, or simply some quick, tasty biscuits for afternoon tea, there is a recipe in this collection for every occasion. The range includes cheesecakes, crunchy shortbreads, cakes featuring fruit, and ever-popular chocolate delights. The wide variety of styles and flavours offers scope for beginners and experienced bakers alike. It is also useful to remember that all of the basic recipes can be adapted according to your preferences and to what you have to hand. For example, sugar can be reduced; sultanas, raisins or cherries can be substituted for dates; any number of spices such as ginger, cinnamon and nutmeg, can be experimented with; and fat-free spreads can be substituted for butter.

Baking tea-time treats is very rewarding. Try your hand at these mouth-watering recipes, and surprise your family and friends with your wonderful new repertoire.

Cherry and Nut Cake

Quantities for 1 28cm/11in
springform tin
500g/1lb 2oz cherries
150g/5¹/₂oz softened butter
150g/5¹/₂oz sugar
4 eggs
100g/4oz plain chocolate
200g/7oz ground hazelnuts
4 tbsps sponge cake crumbs or
digestive biscuit crumbs
1 tbsp icing sugar

Preparation time:
25 minutes
Baking time:
1 hour
Nutritional value:
Analysis per slice, approx, if
divided into 12 slices:
• 1590kJ/380kcal
• 7g protein
• 27g fat
• 26g carbohydrate

Rinse, dry and stone the cherries. • Cream the butter and sugar. Separate the eggs. Grate the chocolate. Whisk the egg whites until they form stiff peaks. Add the egg yolks one at a time to the creamed butter. Add the chocolate and ground hazelnuts. Fold in the whisked egg whites. • Heat the oven to 180°C/350°F/Gas Mark 4. Grease the tin and sprinkle with sponge crumbs or digestive biscuit crumbs. • Spoon the mixture into the tin and arrange the cherries on top. Bake the cake on the lower shelf for 1 hour. • Switch the oven off and leave the cake in the oven for a further 10 minutes. • When cool, sift icing sugar onto the surface of the cake.

Our tip: To make sponge cake crumbs, take some leftover sponge cake bases and leave to dry out in an open tin. Crush with a rolling pin between two sheets of clingfilm.

Strawberry Cheesecake

Quantities for 1 28cm/11in springform tin

For the shortcrust pastry:
200g/7oz flour
Large pinch baking powder
100g/4oz sugar
1 tbsp vanilla sugar
1 egg yolk
100g/4oz butter, diced

For the filling:
500g/1lb 2oz quark, drained
3 eggs
1 egg white
100g/4oz butter
150g/5¹/₂oz sugar
¹/₂ lemon
150g/5¹/₂oz crème fraîche
50g/2oz cornflour
500g/1lb 2oz strawberries
1 packet red jelly glaze
125ml/4 fl oz cream
1 tbsp vanilla sugar

Preparation time:
1 hour
Baking time:
1¹/₄ hours
Nutritional value:
Analysis per slice, approx, if divided into 16 slices:
• 1590kJ/380kcal
• 9g protein
• 22g fat
• 32g carbohydrate

Knead the shortcrust dough ingredients, wrap in clingfilm and leave to chill in the refrigerator. • Separate the eggs. Cream the butter and sugar and add the egg yolks. Grate the lemon rind into the creamed butter and then squeeze in the juice. Stir in the crème fraîche and quark. Whisk the egg whites until they form stiff peaks and then fold them into the quark mixture. Mix in the cornflour. • Heat the oven to 180°C/350°F/Gas Mark 4. • Butter the springform tin. Roll out the dough and use it to line the tin. Bake blind for 15 minutes. • Pour in the quark mixture and bake on the lower shelf for 1 hour. • Rinse, hull and halve the strawberries. • Prepare the jelly according to the manufacturer's instructions. • Arrange the strawberries on

top of the cheesecake and pour
the glaze over them. Allow to
set. • Whip the cream with the
vanilla sugar until stiff, and
pipe a whirl of it in the centre
of the cake.

9

Peach Cake with Almonds

Quantities for 1 26cm/10in springform tin
250g/8oz flour
100g/4oz cornflour
50g/2oz ground almonds
3 eggs
175g/6oz softened butter
Pinch of salt
250g/8oz sugar
2 tbsps vanilla sugar
1kg/2¼lbs peaches
50g/2oz flaked almonds
200g/7oz crème fraîche
½ lemon, rind grated

Preparation time:
1 hour
Baking time:
40 minutes
Nutritional value:
Analysis per slice, approx, if divided into 12 slices:
• 2100kJ/500kcal
• 8g protein
• 26g fat
• 54g carbohydrate

Place the flour, almonds and 50g/2oz cornflour in a bowl. Add one egg, butter, salt, 100g/4oz sugar and 1 tbsp vanilla sugar. Quickly knead to a smooth dough and refrigerate for 30 minutes • Dip the peaches in boiling water, remove the skins, halve and stone them. Bring 250ml/8 fl oz water and 50g/2oz sugar to the boil and simmer the peaches for 15 minutes. • Heat the oven to 180°C/350°F/Gas Mark 4. • Grease the tin. • Cover the base of the tin with the dough, making a 2cm/1in rim. Bake blind for 15 minutes. • Fill the pastry case with the peach halves and sprinkle with almonds. Separate the remaining eggs. Beat the egg yolks with the remaining sugar and vanilla sugar. Stir in the crème fraîche, grated lemon rind and the remaining cornflour. Whisk the egg whites until they form stiff peaks and fold into the egg and cream mixture. • Pour the liquid over the peach halves, smooth the surface and bake for a further 25 minutes. •

10

Leave the cake to cool
completely before removing it
from the tin. Cool on a wire
rack.

Apricot and Quark Crumble

Quantities for 1 baking sheet
500g/1lb 2oz flour
Sachet of dried yeast
250ml/8 fl oz lukewarm milk
75g/3oz sugar
2 eggs
75g/3oz butter, melted
For the topping:
750g/1lb 11oz ripe apricots
750g/1lb 11oz low-fat quark
100g/4oz softened butter
3 eggs
150g/5¹/₂oz sugar
1 lemon, rind grated
1 tbsp lemon juice
Sachet of custard powder
1 tbsp cornflour
For the crumble topping:
125g/5oz flour
50g/2oz sugar
50g/2oz butter
1 tbsp vanilla sugar

Preparation time:
1¹/₄ hours
Baking time:
1 hour
Nutritional value:
Analysis per slice, approx, if
divided into 20 slices:
• 1590kJ/380kcal

• 12g protein
• 15g fat
• 41g carbohydrate

Mix the flour with the dried yeast, milk, sugar, eggs and butter. Cover and leave to rise in a warm place for 30 minutes. • Rinse, dry, halve and stone the apricots. Leave the quark to drain. • Roll out the dough and place on a well-greased baking sheet. Leave for a further 20 minutes. • Cream the butter and sugar. Separate the eggs. Mix the egg yolks into creamed butter. Whisk the egg whites until they form stiff peaks. Add the grated lemon rind, juice, custard powder, cornflour and quark into the butter mixture. Fold in the whisked egg whites. • Heat the oven to 200°C/400°F/Gas Mark 6. • Spread the quark mixture on top of the pastry and then lightly press in the apricot halves. • Bake for 40 minutes. • For the crumble, rub the butter into the flour and sugar and sprinkle over the apricots. Bake for a further 20 minutes.

12

Apricot Cake with Almond Cream

Quantities for 1 baking sheet
500g/1lb 2oz flour
1 tsp baking powder
150g/5¹/₂oz sugar
2 tbsps vanilla sugar
Pinch of salt
2 egg yolks
1 egg
250g/8oz butter
1.5kg/3lbs apricots
250ml/8 fl oz whipping cream
100g/4oz sugar
200g/7oz blanched almonds

Preparation time:
1 hour
Baking time:
45 minutes
Nutritional value:
Analysis per slice, approx, if
divided into 24 slices:
• 1510kJ/360kcal
• 7g protein
• 18g fat
• 42g carbohydrate

To make the pastry, cut the butter into small pieces and knead with the flour, baking powder, sugar, vanilla sugar, salt, 1 egg yolk and 1 whole egg. Place the dough in the refrigerator to chill for 30 minutes. • Rinse, drain, halve and stone the apricots. • Whip the cream until very stiff and then gradually sprinkle in the sugar. Grind 100g/4oz almonds, mix with the remaining egg yolk and mix with the whipped cream. • Heat the oven to 200°C/400°F/Gas Mark 6.• Roll out the dough, place on the baking sheet and prick well with a fork. Lightly press the apricot halves into the pastry, cut-side up and fill each apricot hollow with an almond. • Spread the almond cream on top of the apricots and bake on the lower shelf for 45 minutes.

Pear Slices

Quantities for 1 baking sheet
2kg/4½lbs ripe pears
250ml/8 fl oz water
4 tbsps lemon juice
250g/8oz softened butter
200g/7oz sugar
Pinch of salt
4 eggs
125ml/4 fl oz milk
300g/10oz wholewheat flour
3 tsps baking powder
2 tbsps cocoa powder
200g/7oz ground hazelnuts
200g/7oz apricot jam
1 tbsp apricot brandy
2 tbsps chopped pistachio nuts

Preparation time:
40 minutes
Baking time:
45 minutes
Nutritional value:
Analysis per slice, approx, if divided into 20 slices:
• 1590kJ/380kcal
• 7g protein
• 20g fat
• 42g carbohydrate

Peel, quarter and core the pears and cut them into 1cm/½in slices. Mix the water and lemon juice and pour over the pears. • Cream the butter with the sugar, salt, eggs, milk, flour, baking powder, cocoa and hazelnuts. • Heat the oven to 200°C/400°F/Gas Mark 6. Butter the baking sheet, cover with a layer of the cocoa mixture and smooth with a palette knife. Drain the pears and dry them on kitchen paper and then arrange them in overlapping slices on the dough. • Bake for 45 minutes on the middle shelf of the oven. • Sieve the apricot jam into a bowl, mix with the brandy and warm through. • Brush the jam over the pears and sprinkle with chopped pistachios.

Strawberry Meringues

Quantities for 8 meringues
3 egg whites
200g/7oz sugar
1/2 tsp lemon juice
500g/1lb 2oz small strawberries
20g/¹/₂oz plain chocolate
250ml/8 fl oz whipping cream
1 tbsp vanilla sugar

Preparation time:
30 minutes
Baking time:
2 hours
Nutritional value:
Analysis per meringue, approx:
• 1210kJ/290kcal
• 6g protein
• 12g fat
• 36g carbohydrate

In a bowl which is free of any trace of grease, whisk the egg whites until stiff. Sprinkle them with 150g/5¹/₂oz sugar. Add the lemon juice and beat until the sugar has dissolved. Whisk the meringue mixture again until it forms stiff peaks. Quickly fold in the rest of the sugar. • Line a baking sheet with non-stick baking paper. Use a pencil to mark out eight circles about 8cm/3ins in diameter. Spoon the meringue mixture into a piping bag fitted with a star nozzle. Pipe a spiral base starting from the centre of each circle and then finish with a ring of whirls around the rim. Repeat for the other circles. • Place the meringues in a cold oven on the middle shelf. Dry rather than bake them for 2 hours at 80°C/180°F to 100°C/212°F or Gas Mark ¹/₄. • Remove the non-stick baking paper. • Rinse, dry, hull and halve the strawberries. Grate the chocolate. Whip the cream with the vanilla sugar until stiff and add the grated chocolate. Attach a star nozzle to a piping bag. Fill the bag with the chocolate cream and pipe a cream base on to the meringues. Arrange the halved strawberries in a circle on the cream.

Crumble Cheesecake

Quantities for 1 28cm/11in springform tin

For the crumble:
250g/8oz flour
125g/5oz each sugar and butter
1 tbsp vanilla sugar
1 egg yolk
½ lemon, rind grated

For the cheese filling:
1kg/2¼lbs curd cheese, cottage cheese or quark
125g/5oz softened butter
150g/5½oz sugar
4 eggs
1 egg white
1 tbsp vanilla sugar
½ lemon, rind grated
2 tbsps semolina
Sprinkling of semolina for tin

Preparation time:
50 minutes
Baking time:
1 hour
Nutritional value:
Analysis per slice, approx, if 1 cake is divided into 12 slices:
• 2100kJ/500kcal
• 19g protein
• 23g fat
• 52g carbohydrate

To make the crumble, rub the butter into the sugar, flour, vanilla sugar, egg yolk and grated lemon rind . • Heat the oven to 200°C/400°F/Gas Mark 6. Butter the springform tin and sprinkle with semolina. • Place two thirds of the crumble in the tin and press down lightly. Chill the remaining crumble mix until you are ready to use it. • Squeeze any liquid from the curd cheese, cottage cheese or quark. Cream the butter with the sugar. Separate the eggs. Mix the egg yolks with creamed butter. Whisk the egg whites until they form stiff peaks. Stir the vanilla sugar, grated lemon rind, quark and semolina into the butter and egg mixture. Fold in the stiff egg whites and pour into the tin. Smooth the surface and sprinkle with the rest of the crumble. • Bake for 1 hour.

American-style Cheesecake

Quantities for 1 26cm/10in
springform tin
10 rusks or 5 digestive biscuits
(100g/4oz)
2 tbsps sugar
40g/1¹/₂oz butter
600g/1lb 6oz full fat cream
cheese
200g/7oz sour cream
5 eggs
175g/6oz sugar
¹/₂ lemon, rind grated
2 tbsps lemon juice
50g/2oz cornflour
1 tsp baking powder

Preparation time:
45 minutes
Baking time:
1¹/₂ hours
Nutritional value:
Analysis per slice, approx, if
divided into 12 slices:
• 1680kJ/400kcal
• 12g protein
• 25g fat
• 28g carbohydrate

Wrap the rusks or digestives in clingfilm and crush them with a rolling pin. Rub in with the sugar and butter to make a crumbly mixture. Press the mixture into the base of a tin and smooth the surface. • Combine the cream cheese and sour cream. Separate the eggs. Stir the egg yolks into the cream cheese mixture, together with the sugar, grated lemon rind and juice. Whisk the egg whites to form stiff peaks. Combine the cornflour and baking powder and sift over the cheese mixture. Fold in the beaten egg whites. • Heat the oven to 150°C/300°F/Gas Mark 2. • Spoon the cheesecake mixture over the rusk base, smooth the surface and bake on the bottom shelf for 1¹/₂ hours, until golden brown. • Leave in the oven for 30 minutes, then for another 30 minutes with the door wedged ajar. Open the springform tin and loosen the rim of the cake with the blade of a knife. Do not unmould until ready to serve.

French Orange Cake

Quantities for 1 26cm/10in
springform tin
4 eggs
175g/6oz sugar
1 orange
75g/3oz each flour and
cornflour
½ tsp baking powder
75g/3oz butter, melted and
cooled
50g/2oz flaked almonds
250ml/8 fl oz freshly
squeezed orange juice
Juice of 1 lemon
1 tbsp sugar
2 tbsps icing sugar

Preparation time:
30 minutes
Baking time:
50 minutes
Final preparations:
10 mins
Nutritional value:
Analysis per slice, approx, if
divided into 16 slices:
• 750kJ/180kcal
• 4g protein
• 8g fat
• 22g carbohydrate

Separate the eggs. Beat the yolks with the sugar. • Wash the orange in hot water and grate the rind with a zester. Mix with the flour, cornflour and baking powder and combine with the beaten egg yolks. Whisk the whites to form stiff peaks. Fold into the flour and egg mixture, together with the lukewarm butter. • Heat the oven to 180°C/ 350°F/Gas Mark 4. Line the tin with buttered non-stick baking paper. Sprinkle with the flaked almonds. • Pour the mixture into the tin and smooth the surface. Bake for 50 minutes until golden brown. Switch off the oven and leave the cake to stand for 10 minutes. • Strain the orange juice and mix with the lemon juice and sugar. Warm the liquid through. • Invert the tin and remove the paper. Make a number of holes in the surface of the cake with a thin skewer and pour the juice over it. • Dust with icing sugar prior to serving.

Tyrolean Chocolate Cake

Quantities for 1 30cm/12in
loaf
200g/7oz almonds
150g/5¹/₂oz plain cooking
chocolate
200g/7oz softened butter
200g/7oz sugar
6 eggs
125g/5oz flour
1 tsp baking powder
2 tbsps rum
200g/7oz chocolate cake
covering or icing
Sprinkling of breadcrumbs

Preparation time:
45 minutes
Baking time:
1 hour
Nutritional value:
Analysis per slice, approx, if
divided into 15 slices:
• 1800kJ/430kcal
• 9g protein
• 30g fat
• 29g carbohydrate

Grind the almonds in a mill.
Grate the chocolate. •
Cream the butter and slowly
add the sugar. Separate the
eggs. Add the yolks, one at a
time, to the creamed butter.
Mix the flour and baking
powder and sift into the
creamed butter, together with
the ground almonds and grated
chocolate. Whisk the egg
whites until they form stiff
peaks and fold into the cake
mixture, together with the
rum. • Heat the oven to
180°C/350°F/Gas Mark 4. •
Butter the tin and sprinkle a
few breadcrumbs on top. •
Pour the cake mixture into the
tin, smooth the surface and
bake on the middle shelf for 1
hour. Test the centre of the
cake with a skewer; if it
doesn't come out cleanly, bake
the cake for another 10
minutes. Switch off the oven
and allow the cake to stand for
a further 10 minutes. •
Unmould the cake and leave it
to cool on a wire rack. Melt
the chocolate cake covering
and pour over the cake.

Walnut Gâteau

Quantities for 1 28cm/11in tin

For the cake mixture:
100g/4oz toasted walnuts
250g/8oz wholewheat flour
25g/1oz cocoa powder
2 tsps baking powder
200g/7oz softened butter
200g/7oz honey
4 eggs
4 tsps rum

For the filling and topping:
200g/7oz walnuts
100g/4oz wholewheat flour
½ tsp ground cinnamon
½ tsp vanilla essence
100g/4oz honey
100g/4oz butter
250ml/8 fl oz milk
3 tbsps walnut liqueur
400ml/15 fl oz whipping cream
2 tbsps raw whole cane sugar
½ tsp vanilla essence
16 walnut halves

Preparation time:
30 minutes
Baking time:
35 minutes
Final preparations:
1½ hours
Nutritional value:
Analysis per slice, approx, if divided into 16 slices:
• 2010kJ/480kcal
• 9g protein
• 33g fat
• 33g carbohydrate

Grind the walnuts and mix with the flour, cocoa and baking powder. • Cream the butter and honey. Add the flour mixture, eggs and rum, a little at a time. • Heat the oven to 180°C/350°F/Gas Mark 4. Grease the tin. • Bake the cake for 35 minutes. • Chop 100g/4oz walnuts, and toast with the flour. Add the spices, honey, butter and milk. Stir until the mixture is firm. • Cut the cake into two layers and sprinkle each with half the walnut liqueur. • Add the remaining liqueur to the filling and then spread this over the bottom sponge. Cover with the top layer and press down lightly. • Leave the cake to cool. • Grind the remaining walnuts. Whip the cream with

the sugar and vanilla until stiff and then add the chopped nuts. Coat the cake with the walnut cream and score it into 16 segments. Decorate with cream and walnut halves.

21

Cornflake Cheesecake

Quantities for 1 24cm/9¹/2in springform tin
100g/4oz butter
150g/5¹/2oz plain chocolate
150g/5¹/2oz cornflakes
¹/2 packet unflavoured gelatine
100g/4oz sugar
2 egg yolks
Juice of 1 lemon
250g/8oz low-fat quark or curd cheese
400ml/15 fl oz whipping cream
350g/11oz stoned sweet cherries
2 tbsps chocolate flake (optional)

Preparation time:
1¹/2 hours
Resting time:
1 hour
Nutritional value:
Analysis per slice, approx, if divided into 12 slices:
• 1590kJ/380kcal
• 9g protein
• 27g fat
• 25g carbohydrate

Melt the butter and chocolate and mix with the cornflakes. • Butter a sheet of non-stick baking paper. Arrange 12 small clusters of cornflakes on the baking paper. • Line the base and the sides of the tin with baking paper. Spoon the remaining cornflake mixture over the base of the tin and press down. Place the clusters and tin in the refrigerator to chill. • Dissolve the gelatine in 125ml/4 fl oz hot water. • Beat the sugar into the egg yolks and then mix with the lemon juice and quark. • Whisk the cream until stiff. • Add a few tbsps of the quark mixture to the dissolved gelatine, then add to the quark mixture together with the whipped cream. • Cover the cornflake base with one third of the quark mixture. Spread the cherries on top and then add the remaining quark mixture. Refrigerate the cake for at least 2 hours. • Decorate with cornflake clusters and chocolate flake, if liked.

Crispy Squares

Quantities for 70 pastries
125g/5oz softened butter
1 egg yolk
100g/4oz caster sugar
120g/5oz flour
100g/4oz blanched almonds
1 egg
5 tbsps raw cane sugar
Butter for the baking sheet

Preparation time:
40 minutes
Baking time:
10 minutes
Nutritional value:
Analysis per serving, approx:
• 180kJ/43kcal
• 1g protein
• 3g fat
• 4g carbohydrate

Combine the butter with the yolk. Sprinkle on the sugar and beat until frothy. • Sift the flour onto the butter mixture and gradually fold in. • Preheat the oven to 200°C/400°F/Gas Mark 6. Butter the baking sheet. • Turn the dough onto the baking sheet, and press with your fingertips until very flat. It will be enough once the dough covers the baking sheet evenly. • Coarsely chop the almonds. • Whisk the egg and brush onto the dough. Sprinkle the almonds onto the dough and sift the raw cane sugar onto the almonds. • Bake for about 10 minutes on the middle shelf of the oven until golden. • While they are still hot, cut the cakes into 3 x 4cm/1¼ x 1½in rectangles and cool on a cake rack.

Our tip: *Instead of using beaten egg yolk to glaze, you can brush the pastries with warmed, strained marmalade before sprinkling with the almonds.*

Petits Fours with Fondant Icing

Quantities for 20 petits fours

For the sponge
5 eggs
150g/5¹/₂oz sugar
Grated rind of 1 lemon
¹/₄tsp salt
75g/3oz flour
50g/2oz potato flour
50g/2oz blanched, ground almonds

For the filling and decoration:
400g/14oz raw marzipan
4 tbsps raspberry liqueur
500g/1lb2oz apricot jam
125ml/4 fl oz milk
400g/14oz icing sugar
4 tbsps raspberry jam
10 crystallised violets
30 silver sugar pearls
Non-stick baking paper for the baking sheet

Preparation time:
30 minutes
Baking time:
12 minutes
Standing time:
2 hours
Completion time:
1¹/₄ hours

Nutritional value:
Analysis per serving, approx:
- 1600kJ/380kcal
- 5g protein
- 9g fat
- 65g carbohydrate

Preheat the oven to 200°C/400°F/Gas Mark 6. Line the baking sheet with non-stick baking paper. • Separate the egg whites from the yolks. • Cream the egg yolks with 4 tbsps warm water, the sugar and the lemon peel. • Beat the egg whites with the salt into stiff peaks and fold into the egg yolk mixture. Mix the flour and the potato flour and sift over the mixture. Sprinkle with the ground almonds and fold the ingredients in lightly. • Spread the sponge filling over the baking sheet. Bake for about 12 minutes on the middle shelf of the oven until golden. • Turn the sponge filling out onto a cake rack and immediately remove the baking paper. Leave to stand for at least 2 hours. • Dice the marzipan, cream it and mix

24

with the raspberry liqueur. • Bring the apricot jam to the boil and strain through a fine sieve. • Cut the cake in half, first across, then lengthways. • Coat all 4 sponge sheets with the apricot jam, then coat 2 of the sheets with the marzipan paste. • Lay the sheets which are coated with only the apricot jam onto those coated with the marzipan paste, so that the uncoated sides of the sheets are uppermost. Cut out an equal number of 3cm/1¼in cubes and triangles from the filled sponge. Then coat them with apricot jam. • Heat the milk. Sieve the icing sugar and add just enough milk for a thick fondant to form. • Strain the raspberry jam through a fine sieve and mix with half the fondant. • Take two forks and put a petit four onto each

one. Hold each petit four over a different bowl, each containing the different coloured fondants. Coat all surfaces except the underside of the cubes with the light-coloured fondant, and the triangles with the pink fondant. Arrange all the petits fours on a cake rack. • Put the remaining portions of icing into separate little cones made from greaseproof paper, and pipe little garlands in alternate colours the thickness of a strand of wool onto the petits fours through the small nozzle. • Put the crystallised violets onto the white petits fours and silver sugar pearls onto the pink ones.

Our tip: *Ready-made fondant icing is also available in vanilla, lemon and chocolate flavours.*

25

Polish Apple Meringue

Quantities for 1 baking sheet
200g/7oz softened butter
250g/8oz sugar
1 vanilla pod
3 eggs
4 tbsps milk
225g/8oz flour
50g/2oz cornflour
2 tsps baking powder
50g/2oz each raisins and currants
3 tbsps rum
750g/1lb 11oz cooking apples
½ lemon
½ tsp ground cinnamon
Generous pinch of ground cloves
100g/4oz chopped almonds

Preparation time:
1¼ hours
Baking time:
45 minutes
Nutritional value:
Analysis per slice, approx, if divided into 20 slices:
• 1090kJ/260kcal
• 4g protein
• 13g fat
• 32g carbohydrate

Cream the butter with 100g/4oz sugar. Separate the eggs. Cut the vanilla pod in half lengthways and scrape out the pith. Stir half of it into the egg yolks and milk and then mix this with the creamed butter. Combine the flour, cornflour and baking powder and then stir into the butter mixture, a spoonful at a time. • Wash the raisins and currants in hot water, drain and soak in the rum. Peel, quarter and core the apples and slice them thinly. Wash the lemon in warm water, scrape off the rind with a zester and sprinkle over the apples. Squeeze the juice from the lemon and mix with the apples, together with the rum-soaked dried fruit, spices and 50g/2oz sugar.• Heat the oven to 200°C/400°F/Gas Mark 6. Butter the baking sheet. • Roll out the dough and lay it on the buttered baking sheet. Spoon an even layer of apple mixture over it. Bake for 25 minutes on the middle shelf of the oven. • Beat the egg whites

with the remaining sugar and vanilla until they form stiff peaks. Add the almonds. Spread an even coating of whisked egg white on top of the apples and bake for a further 20 minutes on the bottom shelf.

27

Ginger Sponge Cakes

Quantities for 100 sponge cakes
250g/8oz butter
200g/7oz caster sugar
¹/₂-1 tsp ground ginger
2 eggs
2 tbsps rum
500g/1lb 2oz flour
1 tsp baking powder
100g/4oz crystallised ginger
Non-stick baking paper for the baking sheet

Preparation time:
1 hour
Baking time:
12 minutes
Nutritional value:
Analysis per serving, approx:
• 200kJ/48kcal
• 1g protein
• 3g fat
• 8g carbohydrate

Cut the butter into small pieces and put into a bowl. Place the bowl over hot water, so that the butter becomes workable. • Cream the butter with the sugar, ground ginger, eggs and rum. • Mix the flour with the baking powder. Sift this onto the creamed mixture and knead in. • Preheat the oven to 200°C/400°F/Gas Mark 6. Line the baking sheet with non-stick baking paper. • Cut the crystallised ginger into cubes of just 1cm/¹/₂in in size. • Shape walnut-sized balls from the dough. Press one cube of ginger into each ball and arrange them on the baking sheet, leaving enough space between each one. Bake for about 12 minutes on the middle shelf of the oven until light golden. • Allow to cool on a cake rack. Serve as fresh as possible.

Spice Bars

Quantities for 30 bars
2 eggs
100g/4oz sugar
2 tbsps rum
1 tsp freshly ground cardamom
1 tsp cloves
1 tsp ground cinnamon
150g/5¹/₂oz flour
Butter for the baking sheet

Preparation time:
30 minutes
Baking time:
15-20 minutes
Nutritional value:
Analysis per serving, approx:
• 200kJ/48kcal
• 1g protein
• 1g fat
• 7g carbohydrate

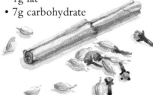

Preheat the oven to 210°C/410°F/Gas Mark 6. Generously butter half the baking sheet. • Beat the eggs with the sugar, the rum and the spices until white and frothy; if using a whisk, allow a good 10 minutes, if using an electric mixer allow about 5 minutes. • Sift the flour onto the creamed mixture and fold in with a wooden spoon. • With a wet palette knife, spread the dough onto the buttered part of the baking sheet. Bake for 10 minutes on the middle shelf of the oven. • Remove from the oven. Cut the cake into 3 x 5cm/1¹/₂ x 2in rectangles, put them back into the oven and bake until the surfaces are well browned. • Cool on a cake rack. Dust with icing sugar if required.

Wholewheat Fig Newtons

Quantities for 100 fig newtons
150g/2oz dried figs, diced
2 tbsps rum
2 tbsps kirsch
100g/4oz shelled hazelnuts
200g/7oz wholewheat flour
1 tsp baking powder and 1 tsp
cream of tartar, combined
1/2 tsp ground cinnamon
50g/2oz candied lemon peel,
diced
50g/2oz candied orange peel,
diced
1/2 lemon
100g/4oz softened butter
3 1/2 tbsps clear honey
2 eggs
50g/2oz raw cane sugar
Juice of 1/2 lemon
Butter for the baking sheet

Maceration time:
1 hour
Preparation time:
45 minutes
Baking time:
20-25 minutes
Completion time:
10 minutes
Nutritional value:
Analysis per serving, approx:
• 140kJ/33kcal
• 24g protein
• 36g fat
• 32g carbohydrate

Soak the figs in the rum and kirsch for 1 hour. • Roast the hazelnuts in a dry pan until the skins burst open. • Rub the nuts in a tea-towel to remove the skins. Then coarsely grind the hazelnuts in a spice-grinder. • Preheat the oven to 190°C/375°F/Gas Mark 5. Line half a baking sheet with non-stick baking paper. • Combine the flour with the baking powder, nuts, cinnamon and candied peels. • Cream the butter with the honey. Gradually combine the flour mixture, eggs and figs with the soaking liquid. • Spread the dough over the baking paper to make a 1cm/1/2in-thick sheet. Bake for 20-25 minutes on the middle shelf of the oven until golden-brown. • For the glaze, boil the raw cane sugar with the lemon juice and a little water

for just 5 minutes, allow to cool a little and brush some over the slab of dough. • Cut the slab of dough into 2cm/³/₄in cubes and allow to cool completely on a cake rack.

Poppyseed and Walnut Striezel

Quantities for 1 28cm/11in
loaf
200g/7oz wholewheat flour
25g/1oz each buckwheat flour
and soya flour
½ lemon, rind grated
20g/½oz fresh yeast or 1 tsp
dried yeast
175g/6oz clear honey
125ml/4 fl oz milk
150g/5½oz walnuts
125g/5oz freshly ground
poppyseeds
Generous pinch of ground
cinnamon
4 tbsps milk
50g/2oz butter
3 tbsps apricot jam

Preparation time:
1¼ hours
Baking time:
30 minutes

Nutritional value:
Analysis per slice, approx,
ifdivided into 16 slices:
• 980kJ/230kcal
• 6g protein
• 13g fat
• 23g carbohydrate

Sift the flours and combine
with the grated lemon rind.
Make a well in the flours,
crumble the yeast into it and
stir in 50g/2oz honey, milk
and about 1 tbsp of the flour.
Cover and leave to rise in a
warm place for 15 minutes. •
Knead the rest of the flour
with the starter yeast and leave
for a further 30 minutes. •
Reserve a few walnuts for
decoration. Grind the
remainder for the filling,
mixing them with the
poppyseeds and ground

cinnamon. Add to the milk and remaining honey. Bring to the boil, remove from the heat and add half the butter. Leave to cool, giving the mixture an occasional stir. • Roll the dough out into a rectangle 30x40cm/12x15in, cover with the filling and roll up, starting from one of the short sides. Cut in half lengthways. • Heat the oven to 200°C/400°F/Gas Mark 6. Butter the tin well. • Wrap the two pieces of dough around each other. Arrange in the tin. Brush the surface with the remaining melted butter and bake for 30 minutes. Test the centre of the cake with a skewer to check whether it is done. Switch off the oven and leave to stand for 10 minutes. Brush the surface with the apricot jam, decorate with the walnuts and leave to cool in the tin.

St Honoré Meringue

Quantities for 1 26cm/10in flan

For the meringue:
4 egg whites
Pinch of salt
200g/7oz sugar
1 tsp vanilla sugar

For the choux paste:
125ml/4 fl oz water
50g/2oz butter
Pinch of salt
75g/3oz flour
2 eggs

For the custard topping:
½ packet gelatine
50g/2oz cornflour
4 egg yolks
500ml/18 fl oz milk
75g/3oz sugar
1 vanilla pod
200ml/6 fl oz whipping cream
2 tbsps orange liqueur

For the sugar syrup:
100ml/3 fl oz water
200g/7oz sugar

Preparation time:
2 hours
Drying time:
5 hours
Nutritional value:
Analysis per slice, approx, if divided into 12 slices:
• 2010kJ/480kcal
• 13g protein
• 22g fat
• 56g carbohydrate

Heat the oven to 100°C/212°F/Gas Mark 1/4. Line the tin. • Whisk the egg whites with the salt, sugar and vanilla sugar, until stiff. Pipe the egg whites over the base of the tin. Dry the meringue in the oven for 5 hours at the lowest setting with the door ajar. • Boil the water with the butter and salt, stirring in the flour. Add the eggs. • Pipe walnut-sized whirls of choux paste onto a buttered tin. Bake for 15 minutes at 200°C/400°F/Gas Mark 6. •

Dissolve the gelatine in 125ml/4 fl oz hot water. Beat the cornflour with the egg yolks and a little milk. Bring the rest of the milk to the boil with the sugar and vanilla pod. Stir in the egg yolk mixture and return to the boil. Remove from the heat and add the gelatine. Whip the

34

cream until stiff. Add the liqueur and mix with the cooled custard and the beaten egg whites. • Pipe custard into the choux pastry whirls. Cover the meringue base with the rest. • Boil the sugar and water in a pan for 5 minutes. • Dip the whirls in the syrup and arrange on the custard topping.

35

Chocolate Cherry Swiss Roll

4 eggs
125g/5oz sugar
75g/3oz flour
50g/2oz cornflour
50g/2oz cocoa powder
1/2 packet unflavoured gelatine
500g/1lb 2oz Morello cherries
350g/11oz mascarpone or full-fat cream cheese
2 tbsps lemon juice
200ml/6 fl oz whipping cream
50g/2oz plain cooking chocolate

Preparation time:
15 minutes
Baking time:
10 minutes
Final preparations:
30 minutes
Nutritional value:
Analysis per slice, approx, if 1 roulade is divided into 10 slices:
• 1380kJ/330kcal
• 13g protein
• 14g fat
• 38g carbohydrate

Heat the oven to 220°C/450°F/Gas Mark 7. Line a baking sheet with non-stick baking paper. • Separate the eggs. Beat the yolks with 3 tbsps water and 75g/3oz sugar. Whisk the whites until they form stiff peaks and fold into the beaten egg yolks, together with the flour, cornflour and cocoa powder. • Pour the sponge mixture onto the baking sheet and bake for 10 minutes. • Dissolve the gelatine in 125ml/4 fl oz hot water. Stone the cherries and chop them finely. Mix with the mascarpone and the remaining sugar. Warm the lemon juice. Add the lemon juice to the dissolved gelatine and then mix with the cherry cream. • Invert the layer of sponge onto a sugared tea-towel. Remove the paper and roll up the sponge. • Whip the cream until stiff, and mix 3 tbsps of it with the partially-set cherry cream. Coat the sponge with the cherry cream, roll up and leave to chill. • Coat the surface with the remaining whipped cream, and grate the chocolate over the top.

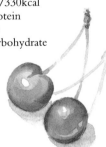

Creamy Peach Swiss Roll

4 eggs
100g/4oz sugar
1 tbsp vanilla sugar
100g/4oz flour
25g/1oz cornflour
500g/1lb 2oz ripe peaches
4 tsps Cointreau
1/2 tsp vanilla essence
2 tbsps sugar
400ml/15 fl oz whipping
cream

Preparation time:
15 minutes
Baking time:
10 minutes
Final preparations:
20 minutes
Nutritional value:
Analysis per slice, approx, if
divided into 10 slices:
• 1380kJ/330kcal
• 8g protein
• 17g fat
• 33g carbohydrate

Heat the oven to 220°C/450°F/Gas Mark 7. • Separate the eggs. Beat the egg yolks with 4 tbsps cold water, sugar and vanilla sugar. Whisk the egg whites until they form stiff peaks. Add the flour and cornflour to the egg yolks and then fold in the egg whites. Line a Swiss roll tin with non-stick baking paper and pour the sponge mixture into it. • Bake for 10 minutes and then invert onto a damp tea towel. Remove the paper. Roll up the sponge layer using the tea towel to help. • Pierce the peaches with a fork and dip in boiling water for a few seconds. Remove the skins and chop the flesh finely, reserving half a peach for the decoration. Soak the chopped peaches in Cointreau. Add the vanilla essence and sugar to the cream. • Whip the cream until stiff and reserve 6 tbsps. Mix the remaining cream with the chopped peach. Coat the sponge slice with the peach cream and roll it up again. • Wrap the roulade in aluminium foil and chill in the freezer for 1 hour. Cut into 10 slices, decorating each with a whirl of cream and a slice of peach.

Buttercream Gâteau

*Quantities for 1 26cm/10in
tin*
5 eggs
Pinch of salt
250g/8oz sugar
125g/5oz flour
125g/5oz cornflour
1 tsp baking powder
*50g/2oz toasted flaked
almonds*
*100g/4oz blanched, toasted
almonds*
125g/5oz sugar
100ml/3 fl oz water
5 egg yolks
250g/8oz softened butter
400g/14oz raspberry jam
*50g/2oz plain cooking
chocolate*
125ml/4 fl oz whipped cream
16 glacé cherries

Preparation time:
20 minutes
Resting time:
1 day
Baking time:
40 minutes
Final preparations:
1 hour
Analysis per slice, approx, if
divided into 16 slices:
• 2390kJ/570kcal
• 12g protein
• 33g fat
• 56g carbohydrate

Separate the eggs and whisk the whites with the salt and 50g/2oz sugar. Beat the yolks with 5 tbsps warm water and the remaining sugar. Stir in the flour, baking powder and cornflour. • Heat the oven to 150°C/300°F/Gas Mark 2. Bake the sponge mixture for 10 minutes. Increase the temperature to 180°C/350°F/ Gas Mark 4 and bake for a further 30 minutes. • Switch off the oven and leave for 15 minutes. • Grind the almonds finely. Boil the sugar and water to a syrup. • Beat the egg yolks and add the syrup. Combine with the almonds and butter, stirring well. • Cut the sponge base crossways into three layers. Coat the bottom two layers with raspberry jam and buttercream. • Replace the top layer and cover the surface and sides with buttercream. Press flaked almonds into the sides and sprinkle the surface with grated chocolate. Pipe with 16 whirls of cream, each topped with a cherry.

Chocolate Cream Gâteau

Quantities for 1 24cm/9 1/2in tin
4 eggs
Pinch of salt
200g/7oz sugar
100g/4oz flour
100g/4oz cornflour
1 tsp baking powder
1/2 packet unflavoured gelatine
400ml/15 fl oz whipping cream
2 tbsps sugar
400g/14oz peach jam
2 tbsps cocoa powder
100g/4oz chocolate vermicelli
100g/4oz candied orange peel

Preparation time:
20 minutes
Baking time:
40 minutes
Resting time:
1 day
Final preparations:
40 minute
Nutritional value:
Analysis per slice, approx, if divided into 12 slices:
• 1800kJ/430kcal
• 7g protein
• 17g fat
• 61g carbohydrate

Prepare a sponge mix as described in the previous recipe using the eggs, salt, sugar, flour, cornflour and baking powder. Bake at 150°C/300°F/Gas Mark 2 for 10 minutes, and at 180°C/350°F/Gas Mark 4 for a further 30 minutes. Leave to rest for 1 day. Cut crossways into three layers. • Dissolve the gelatine in 125ml/4 fl oz hot water. • Whip the cream with the sugar until stiff and stir the dissolved gelatine into it. Place some of the whipped cream into a piping bag. • Spread the two lower sponge layers with jam and cream. Re-assemble the three layers. • Stir the cocoa powder into the remaining cream and spread it over the surface and sides of the cake. Sprinkle with the chocolate vermicelli and dot with whirls of cream, topped with orange peel.

Marzipan Gâteau

Quantities for 1 28cm/11in springform tin
75g/3oz pistachio nuts
300g/10oz almonds
300g/10oz marzipan
650g/1½lbs icing sugar
10 eggs
500g/1lb 2oz softened butter
1 lemon, rind grated
125g/5oz flour
125g/5oz cornflour
200g/7oz lemon curd
200g/7oz plain chocolate couverture or icing

Preparation time:
1 hour
Baking time:
1 hour
Final preparations:
1 hour
Resting time:
7 days
Nutritional value:
Analysis per slice, approx, if divided into 24 slices:
• 2520kJ/600kcal
• 10g protein
• 36g fat
• 56g carbohydrate

Grind two-thirds of the pistachio nuts finely. Dip the almonds into boiling water, leave to cool slightly and then remove the skins. Rub dry and grind finely. • Cut 200g/7oz marzipan into pieces and knead with 100g/4oz icing sugar and the ground pistachios. Divide the marzipan and pistachio mixture into four pieces. • Heat the oven to 250°C/475°F/Gas Mark 9. Butter the springform tin. • Separate the eggs. Cream the butter with 500g/1lb 2oz icing sugar. Add the grated lemon rind and egg yolks one at a time. Combine the flour with the cornflour and ground almonds. Line the tin with non-stick baking paper. Whisk the egg whites to form stiff peaks and fold into the almond and flour mixture. • Use a pastry brush to spread 2 tbsps of the sponge mixture evenly over the tin. Bake on the upper shelf for 5 minutes until golden. • Spread another 2 tbsps of cake mixture on top of

the first layer and bake until golden. Repeat with the third layer. Spread 1 tbsp lemon curd on top. Roll out one of the marzipan and pistachio portions between 2 sheets of clingfilm cut to the same size as the tin. Place on top of the lemon marmalade. Spread 2 more tbsps cake mixture on top. Bake for 5 minutes. • Add another three layers of cake mixture, topped with a layer of lemon curd and marzipan and pistachio mixture. Continue this process until all the cake mixture and marzipan have been used up. When the fourth layer of marzipan and pistachio has been added, bake on the middle shelf of the oven. • Leave to cool and then remove from the tin. Cool on a wire rack. • Brush the surface and sides with lemon curd. • Knead together the remaining marzipan and icing sugar. Roll out a thin layer for the top of the cake and a strip for the sides. Press the marzipan over the cake. • Melt the chocolate icing in a bain-marie and cover the cake evenly, starting from the middle. • Chop the remaining pistachio nuts and sprinkle them over the chocolate icing. • Wrap the cake loosely in aluminium foil and refrigerate for 7 days.

Our tip: *The cake will stay fresh after it has been cut open as long as it is wrapped in foil and kept cool. Its flavour improves with age.*

Devil's Food Kiwi Cake

Quantities for 1 26cm/10in springform tin

For the sponge:
6 eggs
Pinch of salt
150g/5¹/₂oz sugar
100g/4oz flour
50g/2oz cornflour
75g/3oz cocoa powder
1 tsp baking powder

For the filling and coating:
1 packet unflavoured gelatine
4-5 kiwi fruit
50g/2oz icing sugar
600ml/1 pint whipping cream
1 tbsp vanilla sugar
25g/1oz flaked almonds
3 tbsps rum
Butter and dry breadcrumbs for the tin

Preparation time:
20 minutes
Baking time:
30 minutes
Resting time:
1 day
Final preparations:
1¹/₂ hours

Nutritional value:
Analysis per slice, approx, if divided into 16 slices:
• 1510kJ/360kcal
• 9g protein
• 22g fat
• 29g carbohydrate

Heat the oven to 180°C/ 350°F/Gas Mark 4. • Separate the eggs. • Combine the egg yolks with 2 tbsps water and the remaining sugar. Combine the flour, cornflour, cocoa powder and baking powder. Sift this over the egg yolks. Whisk the egg whites with the salt into stiff peaks, slowly adding half the sugar. Fold everything into the egg yolks with a spatula. • Butter the base of the springform tin and sprinkle with breadcrumbs. Pour the mixture into the tin and bake on the middle shelf for 30 minutes. • Release the sponge from the tin and leave to rest for 24 hours, before cutting into slices. • For the cream filling, dissolve the gelatine in 125ml/4fl oz hot

water. Peel the kiwi fruit, reserving one for the decoration. • Chop the other kiwi fruit finely or purée in a liquidiser. Add the icing sugar to the purée and warm through. Whip the cream and vanilla sugar until stiff. Add the whipping cream to the dissolved gelatine a tbsp at a time. Place one third of the cream in the refrigerator to chill. Mix the remainder with the cooled fruit purée. • Chill the fruit cream for 30 minutes. • Toast the flaked almonds in a dry frying pan until golden brown. • Cut the sponge cake twice crossways into three layers. Sprinkle rum over all three layers. Spread the fruit cream on to the bottom and middle layers and then re-assemble the cake. Cover the whole cake with the whipped cream. Attach a star nozzle to a piping bag, fill with the remaining cream and pipe a number of whirls around the top of the cake. Sprinkle the toasted almonds in the centre. Cut the reserved kiwi fruit into slices and arrange them on top of the cream whirls. • Refrigerate the cake until required, but do not store for too long or the otherwise subtle flavours can become too powerful.

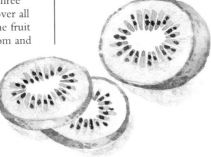

Heavenly Cake

Quantities for 1 26cm/10in springform tin
175g/6oz softened butter
200g/7oz sugar
3 eggs
300g/10oz flour
2 tsps baking powder
100g/4oz ground almonds
3 tbsps vanilla sugar
½ packet unflavoured gelatine
750ml/1½ pints whipping cream

Preparation time:
20 minutes
Baking time:
1 hour 40 mins
Final preparations:
20 mins
Nutritional value:
Analysis per slice, approx, if divided into 12 slices:
• 2390kJ/570kcal
• 10g protein
• 40g fat
• 42g carbohydrate

Cream the butter with 150g/5½oz sugar and eggs. Mix together the flour and baking powder and add to the creamed butter. • Heat the oven to 180°C/350°F/Gas Mark 4. Butter the bottom of the tin. • Spoon a quarter of the mixture into the tin and bake for 10 minutes. • Combine the almonds with 2 tbsps vanilla sugar. Spread a quarter of this mixture over the cake base and bake for a further 15 minutes. • Prepare three more layers in the same way. • Bake the last layer for only 20 minutes and cut it into 12 equal segments. Return to the oven for the final 5 minutes. • Dissolve the gelatine in 125ml/4 fl oz hot water. • Whip the cream with the remaining vanilla sugar and the sugar until stiff. Gradually add the whipped cream to the dissolved gelatine. Transfer a third of the cream to a piping bag. Spread the rest of the cream over the three layers and assemble the cake. • Score the top layer into 12 segments. Pipe a large whirl of cream in each segment. • Arrange the 12 cut segments at an angle on the cream whirls.

Chocolate Nut Triangles

Quantities for 20 triangles:
150g/5¹/₂oz softened butter
150g/5¹/₂oz sugar
1 tbsp vanilla sugar
3 eggs
150g/5¹/₂oz flour
75g/3oz cornflour
1 tsp baking powder
25g/1oz cocoa powder
100g/4oz ground hazelnuts
4 tbsps milk
20 whole hazelnuts
200g/7oz chocolate nut paste
200g/7oz chocolate icing

Preparation time:
30 minutes
Baking time:
20 minutes
Final preparations:
15 minutes
Nutritional value:
Analysis per triangle, approx:
• 1200kJ/290kcal
• 5g protein
• 17g fat
• 30g carbohydrate

Heat the oven to 200°C/400°F/Gas Mark 6. Line a baking sheet with non-stick baking paper. • Cream the butter with the sugar and vanilla sugar. Add the eggs one at a time. Mix the flour with the cornflour, baking powder, cocoa powder and ground hazelnuts and stir into the egg and butter mixture, together with the milk. Pour the mixture onto the baking sheet and bake on the middle shelf of the oven for 20 minutes. • Cut the cake into 8cm/3in squares. • Toast the hazelnuts in dry frying pan and rub off the skins in a tea towel. Warm the chocolate nut paste until it is easy to spread. Melt the chocolate icing in a bain-marie. • Coat half of the squares with the nut paste and then place the remaining squares on top. • Halve the sandwiches diagonally and coat with the chocolate icing. Press the nuts into the warm icing.

Apron Strings

Quantities for 30 apron strings
100g/4oz softened butter
100g/4oz sugar
1 tbsp vanilla sugar
Pinch of salt
3 eggs
3 tbsps milk
500g/1lb 2oz flour
Sachet of baking powder
For frying:
1kg/2¼lbs vegetable cooking fat or 1l/1¾ pints oil
For the coating:
2 tbsps sugar

Preparation time:
40 minutes
Resting time:
30 minutes
Frying time:
about 45 minutes
Nutritional value:
Analysis per apron string, approx:
• 630kJ/150kcal
• 3g protein
• 7g fat
• 17g carbohydrate

Mix the butter, sugar, vanilla sugar, salt, eggs, milk, 3 tbsps water, half the flour and baking powder in a bowl and blend with an electric food mixer at the highest setting for 2 minutes. • Add the rest of the flour and quickly knead by hand to a smooth dough. • Divide the dough in two, wrap each piece in foil and leave to rest in the refrigerator for 30 minutes. • Heat the fat or oil in a deep-fryer or saucepan to 175°C/345°F. The right temperature has been reached if tiny bubbles form around the handle of a wooden spoon when it is dipped into the fat. • Roll out the dough on a floured worktop to a thickness of 4mm/¼in. Use a cutter to cut strips of dough 4x10cm/1½x4ins. Make a small cut about 4cm/1½ins down the middle of each strip. Pull one end of the strip through the incision and open out. • Deep-fry four apron strings at a time, allowing 3 to 4 minutes until golden brown. • Remove the apron strings from the hot fat with a slotted spoon and leave to drain on absorbent paper. Dip in sugar while still warm.

Swiss Squares

Quantities for 40 squares
For the dough:
8 eggs
125g/5oz icing sugar
2 tbsps vanilla sugar
¼ tsp salt
40g/1½oz grated cooking
chocolate
50g/2oz flour
50g/2oz cocoa powder
65g/2oz ground almonds
75g/3oz butter
For the cream:
1 vanilla pod
500ml/16 fl oz milk
40g/1½oz potato starch
3 egg yolks
100g/4oz sugar
250g/8oz butter
3 tbsps kirsch
To decorate:
1 tbsp cocoa powder
50g/2oz flaked milk chocolate
Butter and greaseproof paper for
the baking sheet

Preparation time:
40 minutes
Baking time:
35 minutes

Standing time:
15 hours
Completion time:
1 hour
Nutritional value:
Analysis per serving, approx:
• 780kJ/190kcal
• 5g protein
• 14g fat
• 10g carbohydrate

Preheat the oven to
200°C/400°F/Gas Mark 6.
Butter a 17 x 25cm/6½ x 10in
baking sheet and line with
buttered greaseproof paper. •
Separate the egg yolks from
the whites. • Cream the yolks
with the icing sugar and the
vanilla sugar. • Beat the egg
whites with the salt into stiff
peaks. • Mix the chocolate,
flour, cocoa powder and
ground almonds into the egg
white. Fold this into the yolk
mixture. • Melt the butter over
low heat, but do not allow it
to become hot. Trickle it in a
thin stream into the dough. •
Spread the dough on the
baking sheet. Bake for 35
minutes on the middle shelf of

the oven. • Allow the sponge to cool on the baking sheet. Turn it out on to a work surface and peel off the greaseproof paper. Leave the dough to stand for 12 hours. • About 4 hours before serving, cut open the vanilla pod lengthways, scrape out the pith, and bring to the boil in 375ml/14 fl oz milk. • Stir into the remaining milk the potato starch, yolks and 50g/2oz sugar. • Remove the boiling milk from heat and discard the halved vanilla pods. Add the remaining sugar and then the yolk mixture and bring back to the boil. • Lower the cream filling to room temperature in a cold bain-marie by stirring frequently. • Cream the butter and allow this also to reach room temperature. • Combine the vanilla cream filling and the kirsch with the butter one tablespoonful at a time. • Cut the sponge across twice. Spread each layer evenly with butter filling right to the edges. • Dust the top layer in strips with cocoa powder. Chill for 3 hours. • Before serving, cut the cake into 3 x 3cm/1¼ x 1¼ in cubes and decorate each cube with the flaked chocolate. Arrange the Swiss Squares in sweet cases to serve.

Chocolate Hedgehogs

Quantities for 16 hedgehogs
100g/4oz butter
130g/5oz sugar
¼ tsp salt
200g/7oz flour
1 packet instant chocolate whip
500ml/16 fl oz milk
1 egg yolk
250g/2oz softened butter
200g/7oz icing sugar
2 tbsps drinking chocolate
1 tbsp rum
100g/4oz sponge fingers
100g/4oz almond pieces
300g/10oz chocolate covering

Preparation time:
2 hours
Cooling time:
1½ hours
Baking time:
6-8 minutes
Nutritional value:
Analysis per serving, approx:
• 2050kJ/490kcal
• 6g protein
• 30g fat
• 50g carbohydrate

Knead the butter with 50g/2oz sugar, salt and flour and chill for 1 hour. • Beat the instant whip with 5 tbsps milk and the egg yolk. • Add 2 tbsps sugar to the remaining milk and bring to the boil. Stir in the chocolate whip, bring to the boil and allow to cool. • Cream the butter with half the icing sugar, cocoa and rum. • Dice the sponge fingers. Add the remaining sugar to 5 tbsps water and bring to the boil. Soak the sponges in this. • As soon as the whip has become as cool as the butter mixture, mix them together. Fold in the sponges. Chill the cream filling. • Preheat the oven to 200°C/400°F/Gas Mark 6. Make a 4cm/1½in-long hedgehog-shaped mould out of card. • Roll out the dough, and make 16 hedgehog shapes using the mould. Bake for 6-8 minutes, and cool. • Fill them with the buttercream, and leave to set. Melt the cake covering, cover the hedgehogs with it and add eyes and mouths, and almond prickles.

Deep-fried Mice

Quantities for 32 mice
500g/1lb2oz flour
42g/1¹/₂oz yeast
250ml/8fl oz lukewarm milk
100g/4oz sugar
100g/4oz currants
¹/₄ tsp salt
¹/₄ tsp ground cardamom
¹/₄ tsp cinnamon
Grated peel of ¹/₂ lemon
1 egg
1 egg yolk
50g/2oz softened butter
For coating and decorating:
1 tsp ground cinnamon
4 tbsps sugar
32 blanched almonds
250g/8oz marzipan or string
1l/1³/₄ pints oil for frying

Preparation time:
40 minutes
Standing time:
1 hour
Frying time:
50 minutes
Nutritional value:
Analysis per serving, approx:
• 600kJ/140kcal
• 4g protein
• 6g fat
• 19g carbohydrate

Sift the flour into a bowl. Put the yeast in a bowl, add milk, flour and 1 tsp sugar, and stir. Cover and leave until foaming. Pour the yeast into the centre of the flour. • Wash the currants in hot water, drain and reserve 64 of them. • Mix the remaining sugar, the spices, lemon peel, egg, egg yolk, the butter, the currants and sufficient milk with the first flour mixture to make a kneadable dough. • Cover and allow to rise for 40 minutes. • Divide it into 32 balls and make mouse-shaped ovals. Leave to rise for a further 15 minutes. • Heat the oil to 175°C/350°F in a deep-fat fryer. • Fry 4-5 mice at a time in the hot oil for about 3 minutes until golden. Drain well. • Mix the sugar with the cinnamon and roll the mice in it. Use marzipan or string to make tails. • Make ears from almond halves and eyes from the remaining currants.

Lemon Curd Coins

Quantities for 30 coins
For the dough:
1 lemon
210g/7oz flour
150g/5¹/₂oz butter, cut into
small pieces
100g/4oz sugar
¹/₄ tsp salt
1 large egg yolk
For the curd:
60g/2oz butter
60g/2oz sugar
1 egg
1 egg yolk to glaze
Sugar crystals for decoration
Non-stick baking paper

Preparation and standing time:
1¹/₂ hours
Baking time:
15 minutes
Nutritional value:
Analysis per serving, approx:
• 570kJ/140kcal
• 2g protein
• 8g fat
• 13g carbohydrate

Wash the lemon, dry it and grate the rind. •
Add ¹/₄ tsp rind to the flour, butter, sugar, salt and yolk, and knead to a dough. Wrap in foil and chill for 1 hour. • To make the curd, squeeze the juice out of the lemon. • Mix the juice with the butter, sugar and the remaining lemon peel in a hot bain-marie. • Cream the egg with 1 tbsp water. Add to the butter-and-lemon mixture and beat until creamy. • Chill the curd. • Preheat the oven to 160°C/ 325°F/Gas Mark 2. Line the baking sheet with non-stick baking paper. • Roll out the shortcrust dough as thinly as possible. Cut out circles of 4cm/1¹/₂in diameter. Use a thimble to press little holes in the middle of half the circles. • Arrange the coins and rings on the baking sheet. Brush the beaten yolk onto the rings and sprinkle with the

sugar crystals. • Bake the
pastries for 15 minutes on the
middle shelf of the oven until
golden. Remove them from
the baking sheet. • While they
are still warm, brush the coins
with the lemon curd and place
the rings on top of them.

53

Kumquat Squares

Quantities for 10 squares
300g/10oz frozen phyllo
dough (5 sheets)
12 kumquats
80g/3oz mascarpone (Italian
cream cheese)
2 tbsps honey
1 egg yolk
1 tbsp orange liqueur

Preparation time:
30 minutes
Baking time:
15 minutes
Nutritional value:
Analysis per serving, approx:
• 800kJ/190kcal
• 5g protein
• 12g fat
• 15g carbohydrate

Thaw the phyllo dough. •
Preheat the oven to
200°C/400°F/Gas Mark 6.
Rinse the baking sheet under a
cold tap. • Cut the sheets of
dough once across, so that you
have 10 squares. Using a glass,
lightly mark a circle on each
square. Arrange the pieces of
dough on the baking sheet. •
Wash the kumquats in warm
water, dry them and slice them
into julienne strips. • Mix the
mascarpone with 1 tbsp honey
and brush the mixture over the
circles that have been marked
on the pastry squares. Arrange
the kumquat strips in a star
shape on them. • Whisk the
egg yolk with a little water and
brush some over the edges of
the squares that are not
covered by the kumquat. •
Bake for about 15 minutes on
the middle shelf of the oven. •
Mix the remaining honey with
the liqueur and brush the
kumquats with it.

Palmiers

Quantities for 30 palmiers
300g/10oz frozen puff dough
100g/4oz sugar

Thawing time:
1 hour
Preparation time:
20 minutes
Resting time:
30 minutes
Baking time:
16-20 minutes
Nutritional value:
Analysis per biscuit, approx:
• 210kJ/50kcal
• 1g protein
• 3g fat
• 7g carbohydrate

Lay out five puff dough sheets next to each other on a sugared, floured work surface and leave to thaw. • Before rolling out, sprinkle the surface with sugar again. Roll out a sheet of dough 20x30cm/8x10in, turning the sheet over frequently. Fold in the long sides of pastry to just meet each other. Sprinkle with a little sugar. Cover the dough and leave to chill in the refrigerator. • Heat the oven to 220°C/450°F/Gas Mark 7. Rinse a baking sheet with cold water. • Cut the length of folded dough into strips as thick as a pencil. Place the strips on a baking sheet allowing plenty of room for expansion. Bake for 8 to 10 minutes, turn over and cook for a further 8 to 10 minutes. • Leave the palmiers to cool on a wire rack.

Our tip: *Palmiers taste delicious topped with raspberries and a little sweetened whipped cream. Or try blackberries, cranberry jelly or mango slices. Plain palmiers are delicious with afternoon tea or morning coffee.*

Teatime Puffs

Quantities for 16 puffs
300g/10oz frozen puff dough
100g/4oz sugar
100g/4oz chocolate couverture

Thawing time:
1 hour
Preparation time:
30 minutes
Resting time:
15 minutes
Baking time:
16 minutes
Nutritional value:
Analysis per biscuit, approx:
• 540kJ/130kcal
• 1g protein
• 7g fat
• 16g carbohydrate

Lay out five puff dough sheets next to each other on a sugared, floured work surface and leave to thaw. Roll out to a thickness of about 7mm/¼ in. • Use a cutter or a glass 6cm/2½ins in diameter to make dough circles. On the sugared surface, roll in one direction with the rolling pin, turn over and roll again in the same direction. Rinse a baking sheet with cold water. Place the oval pastry shapes on the baking sheet and leave for 15 minutes. • Heat the oven to 220°C/450°F/Gas Mark 7. • Bake the puffs on the middle shelf of the oven for 8 minutes. Turn them over and bake for a further 8 minutes. • Cool the puffs on another baking sheet. • Melt the chocolate couverture in a bain-marie and dip both ends of each puff in the couverture. Arrange on wire racks and leave until the chocolate has dried.

Our tip: *Alternatively, dip the puffs in coffee fondant icing.*

Chocolate-Coated Batons

Quantities for 100 sticks
200g/7oz flour
1 tsp baking powder
50g/2oz sugar
100g/4oz butter, cut into
small pieces
1 egg
100g/4oz cooking chocolate
Non-stick baking paper for the
baking sheet

Preparation time:
1 hour
Standing time:
1 hour
Baking time:
15 minutes
Completion time:
30 minutes
Nutritional value:
Analysis per serving, approx:
• 97kJ/23kcal
• 1g protein
• 1g fat
• 2g carbohydrate

Combine the flour with the baking powder, and sift into a bowl. Sprinkle with the sugar. • Add the butter to the flour with the egg. Mix these ingredients with a wooden spoon, then knead the mixture with your hands to a firm but elastic dough. • Wrap the dough in foil and refrigerate for 1 hour. • Preheat the oven to 200°C/400°F/Gas Mark 6. Line the baking sheet with non-stick baking paper. • Dust your hands with flour. Make pencil-thick rolls from the dough and cut into 5cm/2in lengths. • Arrange the sticks on the baking sheet. Bake on the middle shelf of the oven for 15 minutes until golden. • Leave the sticks to cool on a cake rack. • Melt the chocolate coating in a small saucepan on low heat or in a bain-marie. • Dip each end of the sticks into the coating and leave to harden on greaseproof paper.

Butter Biscuits

Quantities for 60 biscuits
250g/8oz flour
75g/3oz sugar
¹/₄ tsp salt
2 tsps vanilla sugar
1 egg
125g/5oz butter
For the decoration:
150g/5¹/₂oz icing sugar, sifted
2 tbsps lemon juice
2 tbsps white rum
1 tbsp cocoa powder
2 tbsps sugar strands
25g/1oz candied lemon peel,
finely-chopped

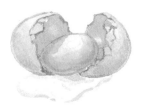

Preparation time:
45 minutes
Standing time:
1 hour
Baking time:
10 minutes
Completion time:
45 minutes
Nutritional value:
Analysis per serving, approx:
• 220kJ/52kcal
• 1g protein
• 3g fat
• 8g carbohydrate

Knead the flour, sugar, salt,
vanilla sugar, egg and
butter, just until they form a
firm dough. Cover with
clingfilm and chill for at least 1
hour. • Preheat the oven to
200°C/400°F/Gas Mark 6.
Butter the baking sheet. •
Divide the dough into four

58

pieces and roll out each in turn to a thickness of 3mm/¼in each. Cut out shapes as desired. Arrange the shapes on a baking sheet. Bake for about 10 minutes on the middle shelf until golden. • Divide the icing sugar into two portions. Add the lemon juice to one portion, and the rum and cocoa to the other. • When the biscuits have cooled, brush one half with one type of icing, and the rest with the other type. Decorate as illustrated.

Cashew Horns

Quantities for 60 horns
80g/3oz cashew nuts
1x2.5cm/1in piece crystallised ginger
110g/4oz butter, cut into small pieces
125g/5oz flour
80g/3oz raw cane sugar
¼ tsp salt
Butter for the baking sheet

Preparation time:
45 minutes
Standing time:
1 hour
Baking time:
15 minutes
Nutritional value:
Analysis per serving, approx:
• 420kJ/100kcal
• 1g protein
• 6g fat
• 10g carbohydrate

Finely grind 50g/2oz of the cashews, chop the remaining 30g/1oz and reserve. • Finely chop the ginger. • Combine the butter with the flour, grated nuts, raw cane sugar, salt and ginger and knead to a firm dough. • Shape 4 equal-sized rolls from the dough. Wrap each one in foil and refrigerate for 1 hour. • Preheat the oven to 175°C/347°F/Gas Mark 3. Line the baking sheet with non-stick baking paper. • Cut each roll of dough into equal-sized pieces. Dust your hands with flour, and shape the pieces into horns on a lightly-floured work surface. Make sure that you do not get too much flour into the dough, otherwise the nuts will not bind into the mixture. Lightly press the upper side of the horns into the chopped cashew kernels. Arrange the horns on the baking sheet and bake for about 15 minutes on the middle shelf of the oven until golden. • Leave the horns to cool a little on the tray, then lift off carefully using a spatula. Allow them to cool on a cake rack.

Honey-and-Almond Biscuits

Quantities for 60 biscuits
200g/7oz wholewheat flour
1 tsp baking powder and cream
of tartar, mixed
100g/4oz softened butter
3¹/₂ tbsps clear honey
¹/₂ tsp vanilla essence
1 egg
100g/4oz blanched almonds,
coarsely chopped
150g/2oz rose-hip jam
sweetened with raw cane sugar
Butter for the baking sheet

Preparation time:
45 minutes
Baking time:
10 minutes
Nutritional value:
Analysis per serving, approx:
• 230kJ/55kcal
• 1g protein
• 3g fat
• 6g carbohydrate

Combine the flour with the baking powder. • Cream the butter with the honey and vanilla. Gradually stir the flour mixture in with the egg. • Preheat the oven to 175°C/350°F/Gas Mark 3. Butter the baking sheet. • Put the chopped almonds in a deep bowl. • Make little oval shapes from the dough and roll them in the almonds. Arrange them on the baking sheet. • Use the end of a pencil to press a hollow into each oval shape. Fill each hollow with some rose-hip jam – for best results, use a piping bag with a suitable nozzle. • Bake for about 10 minutes on the middle shelf of the oven until golden brown. • Leave to cool on a cake rack.

Our tip: *These little biscuits are nice and soft and have only a hint of sweetness. If you want them to taste sweeter add a little more raw cane sugar.*

Shortbread Fingers

Quantities for 40 fingers
200g/7oz sugar
¹/₂ tsp salt
300g/10oz butter, softened
500g/1lb2oz flour
150g/5¹/₂oz caster sugar
Non-stick baking paper for the
baking sheet

Preparation time:
30 minutes
Standing time:
2 hours
Baking time:
20 minutes
Nutritional value:
Analysis per serving, approx:
• 570kJ/140kcal
• 1g protein
• 6g fat
• 18g carbohydrate

Combine the sugar and the salt with the softened butter. • Sift the flour into the mixture. Knead the ingredients quickly into a dough. • Wrap the dough in clingfilm and refrigerate for 2 hours. • Preheat the oven to 190°C/375°F/Gas Mark 5. Line the baking sheet with non-stick baking paper. • Lightly dust a work surface with flour and roll out the shortbread to a thickness of 1¹/₂cm/³/₄in. Lay it on the baking sheet and prick the surface with a fork several times. • Bake for about 20 minutes on the middle shelf of the oven until golden. • While it is still hot on the baking sheet, cut the biscuit into 2¹/₂ x 7cm/1 x 2¹/₂in strips. • Sprinkle the caster sugar on a dish, roll the shortbread fingers in it and allow to cool on a cake rack.

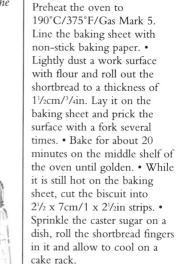

Shrewsbury Biscuits

Quantities for 90 biscuits
440g/1lb flour
150g/5¹/₂oz sugar
2 eggs
¹/₄ tsp salt
¹/₄ tsp ground cinnamon
200g/7oz butter, cut into
small pieces
Non-stick baking paper for the
baking sheet

Preparation time:
30 minutes
Standing time:
2 hours
Baking time:
15 minutes
Nutritional value:
Analysis per serving, approx:
• 180kJ/43kcal
• 1g protein
• 2g fat
• 5g carbohydrate

Sift the flour onto a work surface, and make a well in the centre. Pour in the sugar and the eggs • Sprinkle with the salt and cinnamon. • Sprinkle the butter around the edges of the dough. Quickly knead all ingredients to make a sweet shortcrust dough. • Wrap the dough in foil and refrigerate for 2 hours. • Preheat the oven to 200°C/400°F/Gas Mark 6. Line the baking sheet with non-stick baking paper. • Lightly dust a work surface with flour. Roll out the dough to a thickness of 1cm/¹/₂in and cut out circles 5cm/2in in diameter. • Arrange the biscuits on the baking sheet. Bake for 15 minutes on the middle shelf of the oven until golden brown. Cool them on a cake rack.

Our tip: *Both these shortbreads can be stored in an airtight tin in a cool place for about 3 weeks.*

Index